Table of Contents

Introduction

Before you start your balcony garden, it's significant that you're sure about how much weight the balcony can tolerate. Wet fertilizer and stone or earthenware pots can be shockingly weighty. You might need to select lightweight plastic or gum compartments, in spite of the fact that if your balcony is uncovered and blustery these can get blown over effectively except if they're secured set up.

From the outset, a balcony garden doesn't appear to be any unique in relation to a holder garden. You have a little open air surface and a couple of pruned plants to tell everybody this is the place your home smeets the regular world

It takes a great deal of daylight to develop most vegetables and even those that can endure a touch of shade won't develop well if at all with heaps of it. On the off chance that your balcony is profoundly concealed and you want to develop spices and vegetables you should search out an elective developing space. Discover a plot in a network garden. Persuade your landowner or apartment suite board to let you garden a fix of the yard. Or on the other hand discover a companion or family members open to the possibility of you setting up a little nursery on their property in return for a portion of your collect.

BALCONY GARDENING

When I think of balcony gardens, the first thing that comes to mind is the Hanging Gardens of Babylon. Flowers, vegetables, and herbs cascading over railings softening hard angles and providing food to both the gardener and bees. This is how the mind of a gardener works. Dismissing the minor obstacle of space or aspect, a gardener can envision and create a beautiful space with selected plants and a bit of dirt. The balcony garden can be as big or as small as the mind of the gardener, or the size the space permits. It can range from a few railing baskets to multiple pots and vertical gardens covering every inch of wall space. If you share the gardener's creative mind but are new to the concept, the following steps will ensure a great start to beautifying your space.

How do you start a garden in an apartment or condo? If you have access to a balcony, rooftop, terrace, or patio, you can grow a wide range of veggies, herbs, perennials, flowers, and vines in containers.

Questions to Ask Before Starting a Garden Balcony

A balcony garden can be as complicated or simple as you want. You can spend thousands of dollars or you can make one for very little money. With plant and container choices, you can either make a relatively low maintenance, easy balcony garden or you can do a full-on farm. It depends on your space, light and exposure and the amount of time, energy and/or money you want to spend. Balconies are usually microclimates, differing significantly from the climate on the ground. There can even be different microclimates on a tiny balcony. If an area is shaded, that can be one climate, if another area is exposed to the wind, that is a different climate. The conditions on balconies can be extreme, with huge temperature fluctuations. Also, surface treatments can affect how hot or cool your balcony is and if it retains the heat over time.

The good news is that there are beautiful plants for almost every condition possible. The trick is to really figure out what the environment is before you plan your garden. If you take the time to really evaluate your conditions, your chances of gardening success will be greatly enhanced.

How Big Is Your Space?

Even if your space is microscopic, you can still garden. Fire escapes and windowsills can easily become productive green spaces. It helps to think of your space three-dimensionally. Are there vertical spaces you can plant or hang planters on? Even if there aren't, you can do amazing things to create some vertical space. From piling up pots to creating trellises, there are ways to use all of your space.

How Much Sun Does Your Space Get?

People tend to wildly overestimate how many hours of direct sun a space gets. This is particularly true on a balcony because buildings or walls can obstruct the sun in certain parts of the space. You need to accurately assess how many hours of direct sun each place you want to grow stuff gets. To do this, you will have to either methodically time it out with a watch or get a gardening tool called a sun calculator. You also need to time it close to your growing season, because as the sun moves across the sky, your results will vary from the winter to the summer.

How Much Heat Does Your Space Get?

Again, balconies and rooftops can get searingly hot. Not all plants thrive in extreme heat, so it's best to take this into account when you are planning what to grow. For example, lettuce will not thrive in extreme heat. On the other hand, succulents will be ecstatic.

Is It Windy?

Some plants laugh at the wind and others will curl up and die. It's all about choosing the plants that fit your environment, or to a certain degree, modifying your space to expand your plant pallet. There are ways to create windbreaks to protect more fragile plants by planting larger plants that are wind tolerant in front of the more tender. You can also put plants that don't like the wind in low pots near the floor to give them more protection. Wind dries plants out incredibly quickly, so if your area is windy, you will have to compensate for that by either putting in a drip irrigation system, getting self-watering pots or frequently watering your plants--sometimes several times a day.

How Cold Does It Get on Your Balcony?

The first thing to do is check your "USDA Plant Hardiness Zone." This is particularly important if you want to leave your plants out year round. Given the difficulty of schlepping plants and pots to and from a balcony and the fact that many people look at the balcony all year, it can be a good idea to get plants that will over-winter. That said, your balcony is a microclimate and your zone may be significantly different than a plant growing in a park nearby. Finding your zone is a good place to start when planning your garden. Keep in mind that if you want to leave your plants out through the winter, in cold climates, make sure your plants are rated two zones more cold-tolerant that your area is rated.

How Much Care Are You Willing to Give Your Gardens?

It is a myth that there are "carefree," or "foolproof," plants. Unless they are plastic or already dead, all plants need some care. All plants need water, and most need to be fed. Within that truth, there is a broad spectrum of care requirements and degrees of difficulty and there are ways to minimize the amount of watering and feeding you have to do.

Think about how much attention you want to pay your plants. Are you available and do you want to water what can be several times a day? Do you travel a lot? If you want to or have to minimize your care, there are options. You can install a drip irrigation system, use self-watering pots with large reservoirs, get drought-resistant, low-care plants or even pay someone to water for you. The best idea, if you are just beginning, is to start slowly. See if you like gardening and see how much time you want to spend and how attentive to your plants you are. You can always buy more plants, but if you start slowly, you can get a feel for what works in your space and what doesn't, before you have made too big a commitment.

Do You Have Water Easily Available?

For many balcony gardeners, watering houseplants is an issue. Large pots with thirsty plants can take a huge amount of water and sometimes the faucet is far from the plants. If you have a lot of pots or large pots, you may need to invest in a large watering can that you fill in the bathtub. One of my favorites that would be particularly good for apartment dwellers' plants is the OXO Pour and Store.

Are There Rules About Gardening on Your Balcony?

It is better to know if there are rules against it before you start than have to dismantle your garden after you have built it.

Do You Want to Grow Food?

Edibles can be gorgeous as well as tasty, and the flavor of most homegrown food far outstrips anything you can buy in a supermarket. While you need full sun (six to eight hours of direct sunlight) to grow many vegetables, you can grow lots of greens and some herbs with less sun. Also, many herbs are very easy to grow. By growing your own herbs, you can save money and enhance almost anything you cook.

What's Your Budget?

While it's possible to spend an absolute fortune on a balcony garden, you don't need to. You do need to buy a good quality potting soil, but there are all kinds of ways to minimize what you spend. Try finding pots at yard sales or second-hand stores. Almost anything can be turned into a container, so you might not even have to buy one.

Can any balcony have a garden?

Yes! But don't rush to get it done without some investigation. Wet soil and terra cotta pots are very heavy, so you want to ensure you know the weight restrictions of the balcony before you choose pot materials. Speak with your building manager or a builder to establish the weights you can work with, especially if you have a small balcony. The type of construction material will also determine where the water will go when pots overflow. The neighbors below may not appreciate the rain shower as you water each morning, so consider this issue before a complaint by providing catchment or diversion systems for the containers.

Designing gardens for balconies

Once you have determined the sun aspect and weight limits, you can begin to design your balcony micro-scape. Be creative with the small space by using the wealth of container options different suppliers will have to offer, or by testing the boundaries with your own creative ideas. Design a kitchen garden to grow a portion of your produce or a herb garden for the epicurean. By combining edibles and flowers correctly, you can get the best of both worlds. In your designing stage consider the "thriller, spiller and filler" technique of planting, which incorporates multiple varieties in one pot—the thriller being the focal upright, the spiller to cascade over the pot, and the filler to take up the spaces in between. This design tip uses the beauty of the small garden to add to your exterior home decor.

Thrillers

Tomatoes, peppers, rosemary, snapdragons

Spillers

Strawberries, squash, lobelia, bacopa, nasturtiums

Fillers

Parsley, carrots, basil, amaranth, violets, geraniums

Consider Your Containers

Planters and pots

If weight is not an issue, large planters and pots made of wood or terra cotta are very attractive and offer ample space for all types of growing. Keep in mind that terra cotta usually dries out quickly, however. Resin and plastic pots offer a lightweight alternative in the greatest number of sizes, shapes, and self-watering options. With large pots and planters, the gardener has the opportunity to grow individual small shrubs, perennials, or a wide variety of traditional garden vegetables. Smaller pots and planters are great for planting kitchen herbs, perennials, and annuals. They can be used in combination with vertical gardening.

Vegtrug Balcony Garden Planter

The Vegtrug wall hugging planter is designed specifically for narrow, urban spaces like balconies.

Going Vertical

Vertical gardens are a space saving concept to the home gardener because they employ the vertical walls of your balcony. There are many creative ways to use this method: using pallets filled with soil and affixed to the wall, attaching pots to a trellis, hanging gutters from a chain, or terracing on planter stairs. On the downside, the vertical garden can have a splash factor that can dirty the walls from overhead watering and dripping from a height. Drip irrigation works well to avoid this problem combined with a catchment system at the bottom.

Railing or Hanging Baskets

Railing baskets, window boxes, or hanging baskets are the easiest choices for the tiny balcony. Made of wood, steel, or plastic, these containers are built to hang off the balcony railing or from the eaves. Usually shallow in nature and more prone to dry out, these types of baskets are suitable for drought-resistant plants or those smaller in size. Succulents, annuals, strawberries, herbs, and lettuce can be successfully grown in a railing or hanging basket. Both of these container options should be secured using zap straps, screws, or brackets to prevent the container from being knocked off by wind or an accidental bump.

Up-cycled containers

As a gardener, you are the artist and have the creative licence to explore a variety of containers. To add your own personal flair to the balcony landscape, transform household items into a plant container by adding sufficient holes for water drainage. Up-cycling colourful rubber boots, old yogurt containers, mugs, jugs, baskets or any other vessel is one way to reduce your garbage and also save you money.

Type of Containers And Their Plant Varieties Suitable For Planting

Planters and Large Pots

Boxwood, small conifers, dwarf fruit trees, squash, carrots, rosemary, onions, garlic, citrus, datura, banana, bamboo, Japanese maples, bay laurel, pampas grass, aloe, sensevieria.

Vertical Gardens

Lettuce, strawberries, spinach, basil, parsley, trailing annuals, beans, peas, clematis, honeysuckle, melons, ferns, spider plants.

Railing Basket

Sedum, stonecrop, strawberries, lettuce, marigolds, pansies, petunias, geraniums, basil, parsley, cilantro, thyme.

How to Maintain Small Garden on Your Apartment Terrace

In an age where technology rules our lives, the desire to unplug and get in touch with nature that many of us experience is almost unprecedented. Increasingly, urban apartment dwellers are seeking to grow their own herbs, produce, and even table centerpiece flowers. If you'd like to start your own garden but only have a modest apartment balcony to work with, take these small space design and maintenance tips into account.

Choose Plants Wisely

Before you choose plants and herbs for your garden, identify the parameters you have to work with. Do a little research and find plants you want in your garden that won't grow too high or develop root systems. In addition to selecting space-efficient plants, choose what can thrive in your balcony's climate. Typically, plants that grow well in your area can also do well on your terrace, but some balconies have microclimates of their own. Take a look at how sun exposure, humidity levels, wind, and temperatures vary to those that prevail in the streets, parks, and neighborhoods around your apartment.

Some examples of plants that can do well on balconies include basil, blueberries, currants, rosemary, and tomatoes. Vine plants are great because they take up little horizontal space. Where flowers are considered, perennials such as veronica, Russian sage, and aster are easy to grow in many parts of the country and can be picked for table centerpieces and apartment decor. If you want to grow herbs consider rosemary, cilantro, parsley, thyme, and many other herbs which can be maintained mess-free in mason jars in your kitchen or on your balcony.

Get Creative with Planters

Once you decide what to plant, the next step is to choose the containers. Select pots, planters, and other containers that can accommodate the plants you choose and work well with the design of your space. Tiered planters are great for balcony gardens not only because they can help you make the most of your space but they can also make watering more efficient.

Maximize Sun Exposure

With the exception of plants that do better in the shade, arrange your garden in a way that maximizes the sun exposure each plant gets. Depending on the layout of your balcony, it may be best to line the perimeter of it with plants or to concentrate them in one area. If you do the latter, arrange plants by height so tall plants don't block smaller plants from getting sunlight. Or elevate rows of plants that are further from the balcony's edge. Frequent container rotation may be necessary to help your plants get the sun they need to survive.

Establish a Plant Care Routine

Streamlining your garden with plants that have similar watering requirements will make it easier to stick to a routine. If you do choose plants with different watering requirements, consider arranging them into sections to make plant management easier.

In addition to watering and planter rotation, remember to fertilize your plants as needed. Once every two or three weeks, you should remove faded flowers and any weeds that have managed to crop up in your planters. You can also prune branches that appear unhealthy or overgrown to keep your garden compact and free of plant disease.

Don't Overdo It

Whatever plants you pick and however you choose to arrange them, it's important to leave some space for yourself. If you want a hammock or a table and chairs on your balcony, make those a priority. Having fewer plants competing for space and sunlight on your balcony may help them thrive. It also prevents clutter on your balcony and makes garden maintenance easier.

Follow these tips, and you should be able to make a hobby out of gardening on your apartment balcony regardless of its size. If you want to tend to a more comprehensive garden that contains plants you can't easily grow on your balcony, check out community gardening options in your area.

Gardening is a therapeutic activity that helps you start or end your day in a calm and natural environment. It also enables you to experience the gratification of preparing healthy meals with ingredients you have grown yourself.

Preventing Pests in Your Garden

Encourage Beneficial Insects.

While pollinators are great to have in the garden, the beneficial insects I'm talking about here are those that take a literal bite out of pest insects. Ladybugs, lacewings, minute pirate bugs, parasitic wasps, damsel bugs, and other beneficials naturally help keep pest numbers down by eating the bad guys for lunch or using them to house and feed their developing young. To attract these good bugs to the garden, you need to supply them with protein-rich pest insects to consume as prey, as well as carbohydrate-rich nectar. But, not just any flower will serve as a nectar source for beneficial insects. They need a special type of floral architecture from which to source nectar. Here is a list of some of the best plants for beneficial insects. The more pest-munching beneficials you have around, the less likely it is for pest numbers to get out of hand. It's all about creating a good balance. If you want to know more about how to attract beneficial bugs to your garden, here's an excellent guide. Beneficial insects are great at preventing pest outbreaks. Attracting beneficial insects, like this ladybug, to your garden is a great way to prevent garden pests from taking hold.

Choose Your Plants Wisely.

Some plants and plant varieties are more prone to pest issues than others. Preventing pests in your garden is sometimes as simple as choosing pest-resistant vegetables. For example, if squash bugs constantly plague your winter squash plants, 'Butternut' and 'Royal Acorn' are two of the most resistant varieties. Or, if Colorado potato beetles always try to defoliate your potato crop, plant 'King Harry' potato (a variety bred at Cornell University) which has very hairy leaves that the beetles won't eat. Seek out pest- and disease-resistant varieties of other vegetables, too. Prevent squash bugs by choosing resistant varieties. Variety selection goes a long way toward preventing squash bugs. Young plants can also be covered with floating row cover until they come into bloom.

Employ Physical Barriers.

One of the most useful methods of preventing pests in your garden is to put a physical barrier between the plant and the insect. Cover pest-susceptible plants with floating row cover, a lightweight, spun-bound fabric that rests on top of the plants or on wire hoops. Make sure there's plenty of slack in the cover and pin the sides to the ground to keep sneaky pests from crawling under the edges. I use row cover to keep imported cabbageworm caterpillars off my cabbage, broccoli, and kale. I also cover my young bean plants to prevent Mexican bean beetles, my young cucumber plants to keep cucumber beetles at bay, and my young squash plants to deter squash beetles and vine borers. Just remember to remove the row cover when the plants come into flower to allow access to pollinators. Use floating row cover to prevent pests from attacking plants. Prevent garden pests by covering plants with floating row cover.

Utilize Intercropping.

Preventing pests in your garden can also be the result of increasing the diversity of your vegetable patch. By inter-planting different vegetable crops with each other – and with flowering herbs and annuals – pests may have a more difficult time locating their host plants. Rather than planting a single crop in a row or block, mix everything up to keep even small monocultures out of the garden. Though there's much research still taking place regarding exactly how intercropping works, it appears that this technique "confuses" the pest insect. In order to locate and confirm that a particular plant is a suitable host, some pests may have to land on the plant a certain number of times. When crops are interplanted, the pest might land on a different plant species every time, making it harder for the bug to hone in on its dinner. Dill is an excellent crop for attracting beneficial bugs. Plants with small flowers and fragrant foliage, like this dill, are excellent plants for intercropping and attracting beneficial insects.

Grow Healthy Plants.

It may seem like a no-brainer, but in this horticulturist's opinion, this is the most important method of preventing pests in your garden. Just like you and I, plants have an immune system (albeit one that's quite different from our own), and when plants are healthy and un-stressed, they're naturally less attractive to pests. Plus, healthy plants have a whole host of cool tricks for deterring pests through the use of their own chemical defense system (you can read more about that amazing stuff here). The healthier your plants are, the better able they are to fight off pests all on their own. Feed your plants by feeding your soil a healthy diet of organic matter and make sure they're planted in conditions where they'll thrive (sun plants in sun, shade plants in shade, etc.). Raising happy, healthy plants is one of the easiest steps toward preventing pests in your garden. By employing these five strategies in your vegetable garden for the long-term, you'll be able to gain a good balance between good bugs and bad, and you'll have fewer pest outbreaks as a result.

5 Benefits of Having a Balcony Garden

1. Connect with Nature

Balcony gardens are for those who love the feel of nature in their home. From vertical gardens to potted plants to creepers to hanging plants, options are in abundance to set up a perfect balcony garden and to relax and unwind in the company of nature.

2. Ambience

A touch of greenery in your apartment make the interiors highly appealing and also induces a refreshing feel. Not to mention, having flowering plants or greens adds to the magical charm.

3. Healthy Living

A balcony garden acts as a filter for the stale and polluted air entering the apartment and encourages the flow of fresh air which benefits healthy living.

4. Fresh Produce

Growing a balcony garden will provide access to fresh produce even if in small quantities. It can be the go-to source for herbs and vegetables like tomatoes, chillies, beans etc.

5. Gardening

For those who hail gardening as their favourite hobby, a balcony garden is the ideal option to encourage their green thumb.

Featuring exclusive balcony gardens for all apartments, Melonwood Greens, flagship project of Melonwood Homes upholds the principle of living with nature in the heart of the city.

What Can Your Balcony Garden Grow?

In general, herbs are relatively easy to grow and plants that have vines take up little space because they can grow vertically. Here are some of the plants that are most likely to grow easily on a balcony:

Cucumbers

Tomatoes

Peppers

Zucchini

Summer squash

Celery

Lots of greens (lettuce, kale, mustard's, spinach, bok choy, etc)

Broccoli

Mint

Rosemary

Cilantro

Lavender

Parsley

Basil

Tarragon

Radishes

Spring onions

Herbs tend to like full or partial sunlight (at least four hours), so consider positioning them on the sunniest part of your balcony. You could also keep them inside by a window and leave the balcony for the plants that require bigger pots and a little bit more space. Most greens, on the other hand, can thrive in the shade, as can root vegetables.

The Layout of the Garden

The layout of your garden will ultimately depend on where the sunniest spots are, how much furniture you have on the balcony, how much space you need for entertaining guests, and how you can arrange your containers in a way that allows you to still walk around and water them with ease. Another tip is to layer your plants with the tallest toward the back, near a wall, with the shorter ones in front. It's easier to water them and more aesthetically pleasing.

Planting Your Fruits and Veggies

1. Always arrange your containers before you pour the soil. They're much lighter and easier to move that way.

2. Pour in your organic potting soil and mix in a little organic fertilizer.

3. Plant your seeds or seedlings only as far down in the soil as recommended.

4. Add more soil around the base of the seedlings if necessary, once all the plants are in place.

5. Add water until the soil is wet, but not completely saturated, and be sure to keep the water off the leaves as the plants grow.

What You Need, Other Than the Seeds

1. Pots, appropriately sized for the amount of root space the plants will need (Life on the Balcony has a helpful post about choosing the right pots)

2. Materials for vines to climb

3. Hanging baskets or troughs (optional, but they can help utilize your space since they won't be on the floor)

4. Gloves for keeping your hands clean and unscratched

5 Trowel for digging

6 Watering can (the more plants you have and the more water they need, the bigger the watering can should be so you can be more efficient)

7. Soil

8. Organic fertilizer

Flowers for Balcony Gardens

Flowers that thrive in alpine or rock gardens are also ideal candidates for balcony gardens. Like alpine environments, balconies are exposed to unbuffered winds, and the succulent leaves and low profile of these flowers protect them from desiccation and breakage. Alpine flowers also get by on less water, making them low maintenance and less likely to drip on neighbors below. Include Armeria sea pink for a cushion of bright pink flowers in late spring. Delosperma hardy ice plant produces daisy-like flowers over a long period. Dianthus flowers will cheer you up with a spicy fragrance. The penstemon may attract passing bees and butterflies. If you aren't ready for the commitment of perennials, choose drought-tolerant annuals that don't need fussing to thrive. Vinca flowers are self-cleaning; no need to deadhead. Million bells are petunia look-alikes but won't look like something the cat dragged in after a rainstorm.

The small space of a balcony garden makes pest control methods that are usually laborious seem feasible. Handpicking is a viable way to control any insect large enough to be handpicked! Put on your gloves, and drop all offending beetles, caterpillars, and slugs into a bucket of soapy water. Nip pests in the bud early, as infestations blossom quickly in such a small area.

As you prune and groom your balcony garden, think about buying a kitchen composter so you can turn clippings and veggie scraps into black gold for your plants. Bokashi models promise quick results with no smell. When winter arrives, balcony gardeners must decide how or whether to save plants. For the gardener with annuals, it's fun to start with fresh specimens each year. If some of the flowers are expensive exotics, you may be able to overwinter them in a sunny window. Hardy perennials may survive the winter in their containers; large containers with excellent drainage are the key to success here. Finally, you can take cuttings or divisions of large perennials to overwinter indoors. This challenge is part of the fun of balcony gardening.

Balcony gardening is the practice of growing plants, including edible plants, exclusively in containers instead of planting them in the ground A balcony garden might be small, enclosed and usually portable object used for displaying live flowers or plants. It may take the form of a pot, box, tub, pot, basket, tin, barrel or hanging basket.

Edible Balcony Garden Ideas

You haven't got a lot of it, so make the most of your space. Turn the garden on its side by planting up vertical spaces instead. This could be as simple as training climbing beans or cucumbers up trellis, or securing window boxes to railings.

Walls are a blessing. Use them to mount planters to create a wall of green, or set up any number of wall-mounted or stackable modular planters aimed at the urban gardener. You could also use shelving to create a 'plant theater' of herbs or strawberries. Make sure to fix the shelving securely to the wall so it can't blow over.

Don't forget hanging baskets and other suspended planters at head level. With plants growing up from below and trailing down from above, it's possible to create the illusion of a lush, bountiful garden far bigger than the modest footprint of your balcony. You will want to sit back and admire your handiwork from time to time, so don't sacrifice somewhere to unwind at the expense of squeezing in yet more plants. A small patio table and chair set offers somewhere outside to do the crossword, enjoy breakfast or sip a sundowner.

Best Balcony Garden Plants

Hardy aromatic herbs tolerate the exposed conditions of a balcony, so incorporate the likes of rosemary, lavender and thyme. In fact, all herbs are a wise choice given their high value and their low space requirements, and they will give you something to pick almost every day of the year. Containers supporting edibles such as salad leaves, cherry tomatoes and miniature varieties of vegetables including beets and compact summer squashes are fun to grow and deeply rewarding. Opt for quick-to-mature crops and there's no reason you can't get two, three or even four harvests from the same pots each year. And don't forget to include some flowers to help draw in pollinators and keep pests under control.

Above all a balcony garden should be a refuge a bolt hole to commune with passing nature and decompress after a long day. Get creative, be ingenious and you can grow your very own garden in the sky.

Conclusion

Planning ahead is perhaps the most important tip in your guide to a quick and easy balcony garden. You'll need to take space and the amount of sunlight the area gets, of course, but you should be realistic about how much time and energy you want to commit to your garden so you're not disappointed or overwhelmed.

Instead, you can celebrate your health and the delicious food you're growing right outside your door!

www.ingramcontent.com/pod-product-compliance
Ingram Content Group UK Ltd.
Pitfield, Milton Keynes, MK11 3LW, UK
UKHW022008190726
13853UKWH00004B/1807

9 798505 910924